ANDY

AND

THE GOLD MINE

By Georgette Baker

Photographs by Georgette Baker
Photos altered by Georgette Baker

Story written by Georgette Baker
as told to me by Andy

Cover by Evelyn Quijas

Cantemos San Diego, CA
email: bakergeorgette@yahoo.com

Audio book available on amazon.com

www.cantemosco.com

CHAPTER 1

The air choked me with its heat and dust as we pulled up to Randsburg in the summer of 1962. It was going to be another dreary summer in this small ghost town in the high Mojave Desert in California, hot, dusty and boring.

There were no ghosts here; they only called it a ghost town because no one lived here anymore, it was practically abandoned. If there had been ghosts that would have been something but from past summers, I knew there was nothing interesting about Randsburg. I was the only kid my age in this parched, barren town, the rest of the kids were either babies or too old to want to play with me. At 10 years old there were other places I would have liked to be.

Mom parked the car, a Lark Station wagon Studebaker, in front of the two bedroom house we

rented every summer. We both got out and pulled out boxes full of stuff for sale in Mom's shop. With arms loaded, we headed in the direction of the old bank building, Mom's shop was next to the antique dealer's junk shop. I stepped aside quickly as large tumbleweed. rolling on a gust of wind, threatened to knock me over. I could see the El Paso Mountains in the distance as I helped Mom carry in the curios and pottery she sold to tourists during the summer.Money was tight since Dad had died in an airplane accident and Mom, a teacher during the school year, supplemented her income by selling knick knacks to hobbyist history buffs or day trippers traveling Highway 395. "There are several gold mines here," Mom said, trying to cheer me up. "Maybe you could go down and see how they get gold out of the rocks."

"Aww Mom, What would I do with gold?" I asked trying to show little interest.

"Why, William Andrew Cherry! What would you do with gold? Take it down to the Merchant Store and buy yourself a Nehi and a Moon Pie!" Mom answered looking at me sternly and trying not to laugh. She only called me William Andrew when she wanted me to pay attention, otherwise she called me Andy.

"How will I know which way to go?" I mumbled as I swerved out of the way of yet another prickly, rolling plant remnant.

"Just go down to the General Store and ask Mr. Baker where the Butte Mine is. But Andy, please help me unload the car first."

I went back to the car and picked up a box of tiny paintings Mom had done and framed. I looked at the name at the bottom, "Esperanza", my Mom's name was "Hope" but she always signed it in Spanish, "Esperanza". She loved languages and I guess preferred her name in another language, I'd have to ask her sometime. I put the books on the glass case at the entrance of the shop.

"Thanks son, you're a big help. I'll see you later. I'm going to make you chicken fried steak and biscuits for dinner so don't be late.

Oh and Andy, take your flashlight and a canteen or water bottle!"

"Yes ma'am," I said ruefully. "How much was I supposed to carry around?" I thought to myself. I grabbed an old canteen with a strap that was hanging on a nail in the shop, filled it with some cool water from the sink in the store bathroom. I walked back to the house and dug my flashlight out of the glove compartment of the old, tan, Studebaker, now covered with a film of fine dust. I went back in the direction of the shop and waved to Mom. Her face lit up as if I'd given her a present. Mom was goofy that way. I then headed towards the General Store.

I scuffed my tennis shoes on the dirt road, kicking up a stone now and then, as I made my way down the irregular series of crooked streets passing familiar wooden buildings. I would look at the **Superman** comic books and decide which one I would buy if I found some gold.

Tall piles of mining tailings and rusty, old equipment littered the landscape like old dinosaur bones. The few houses of adobe, stone, and wood stood with curtains blowing through open windows. Dust lifted them in

the air as the wind whipped down the street ahead of me. The air was hot and my lips were dry.

The General Store was a wooden building with a maroon painted façade. Two large windows on each side of the wooden door provided light and allowed me to see the goods inside the store. The words, "*General Store*" were painted across the front of the store above the windows and door and "*soda fountain*" was written above that. The double wooden screen doors banged noisily behind me as I entered. Inside, it was dark and cool; a long soda fountain counter dominated the left side of the store. Brown, cushioned, swivel stools stood empty. I could smell the sweet syrups used to make crème soda and egg creams, sarsaparilla, and cherry coke when the phosphate fizzed liquid was added. I could smell my favorite, vanilla coke. On the other side of the room, were cans of beans, boxes of soap powder and other household goods. The cash register, stood on a counter at the front of the store, the gold scale held a prominent position.

At the back of the store, an open cold case had pop in bottles, including the one I preferred, Orange NeHi. The books and magazines of bright colors were displayed neatly on wooden shelves next to the cold case. I drew my eyes away and focused on Mr. Baker, lean and tall, who sat reading a newspaper, wire rimmed glasses perched on his nose. He sat in a chair near the magazine stand.

"Afternoon, Mr. Baker. How're you?" I asked, remembering that I better mind my manners or it would get back to Mom. We lived on a Naval Air weapons Test Center where politeness was mandatory.

"Mornin' Andy, welcome back son, what can I do fer you t'day?"

"Where's the Butte Mine sir?"

"The Butte Mine huh? You gonna spend the gold you find here?"

"Sure." I mumbled "Nowhere else sells

anythin' I want." I answered as I picked up

the latest **Superman** comic book. Mr. Baker laughed as if I had said something funny.

"You know son, the Butte Lode Mining Company was formed in 1899 and produced a total of two million dollars in gold and silver."

"Wow, sure would like to see that much gold!" I said. Mr. Baker grinned. "Wouldn't we all. Now lookee here, this is what you do son. Pass the place called the Joint, you know the place where everyone hangs out; pass the Santa Barbara Church and the old high school. If you look carefully, you'll see the top of Red Mountain and you will be getting closer to the "bang, clink, bang, clank" noise made by the stamping machine at the mine. It will get louder and louder and you know you will be getting closer. Cross over a single, old mine track and you'll run in to a mine sooner or later. Don't forget yer water and a flashlight."

"Yes sir," I answered as I flipped through the latest **Superman**. The cover said, ***"The Last Days of Superman"*** and showed a picture of my favorite comic book hero encased in a huge block of ice, price 12 cents. It might as well have been 12 dollars, where was I going to get 12 cents?

I thanked Mr. Baker and headed out the

swinging doors into the scorching afternoon day. I left, discouraged that I didn't have the money for the latest comic.

CHAPTER 2

I searched the huge piles of dirt ahead, spotted the tip of Red Mountain beyond them and started walking up the dusty road in that direction. I walked for 15 minutes, glancing briefly at the hang out place on my right, past the church; read the hand painted sign, *Santa Barbara Church 1889.* The tall white steeple rose up to the sky like the lance of a knight. Bang, clank, bang, clank, over and over and over, I listened to the quick, monotonous pounding of rocks by heavy hammers. Bank, clank, bang, clank they whirred.

Squinting down to keep the glare out of my eyes, I saw a large, brown tarantula heading towards a small hole in the ground.

I looked around for a stick, glad to have something to do besides walk. The hairy creature quickly crawled into a dark opening between two large rocks. I got down on my knees and peered into the hole. I took my small flashlight out of my jeans pocket and shined it into the aperture. There was the spider, scrunched up, eight legs pulled in tight, fangs glistening reflection from my light. I looked around for a stick, saw none and stood up, looked around again and gave up. Too hot, way too hot to be chasing anything. Bang, clank, bang, clank, the noise reverberated once again in my consciousness. I saw the single, old mine track Mr. Baker had mentioned.

I climbed on the rusting track and balanced myself, arms wide, stepping quickly, never falling, must have gone 15 successful feet when I notice a horned lizard on a wooden plank. The tubby, round-bellied lizard had the fierce look of an angry monster. Horns protruded from all parts of its body. He glared at me, a furious expression on a creature the size of my thumb, I laughed and stepped around it, guffawing at the funny sight it presented and then I tripped, barely avoiding busting my lip open on the jagged rocks in front of me.

"Argh!!! I yelled and looked up from my dusty bed. That's when I saw it.

CHAPTER 3

It was a big, dark, opening in the earth surrounded by wooden slats like the mouth of a giant bird at feeding time, waiting for a body to swallow down. I put my ear on the ground and listened. There was no grumbling from the monster's stomach and no mine noises either. I knew it wasn't the Butte Mine because no one was around working. No not the Butte mine but, my mine, Andy's mine. I could see it now, ten year old boy strikes it rich near Randsburg, California, buys his mother a house and…and what?

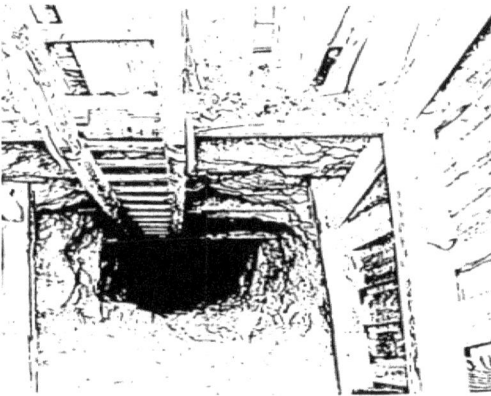

If the mine was mine then I better go over and see what I could find. I got up, dust clung to my clothes.

I secured my flashlight and repositioned my canteen as I walked over to the opening. I peered inside. Tracks, red with rust that had been used to guide the mining carts into the belly of the earth were in place. Wood planks, buckled by sun and heat, were the remains of a ladder. I was going to get the beating of my life if I went down there by myself. No one would ever find me if I fell and got hurt. Those thoughts left faster than they had arrived. This was my mine, Andy's mine and I had to go down and see what I could see.

Squatting and then sitting on the edge of that dark wooden lip so my feet dangled towards the ground, I took the flashlight from my back pocket and watched its rays get swallowed up. I picked up a stone and dropped it in to the dark opening; it wasn't long before I heard it hit the bottom. "Not too deep," I thought to myself.

I could see nothing below. Turning on my stomach and holding on to the first rung of the ladder-like structure, I stepped into the darkness. I reach the bottom quickly, the mine wasn't as deep as it had seemed, my flashlight now appeared brighter and I waved it around. Rocks were piled here and there, the splintered handle of a pick axe carelessly tossed on top of them. A big nothing, no gold shining up from the ground, no gold glistening from the walls. The mine had been blasted shut and it was like a small vertical cave. Big bore, me and an empty cave full of rocks and an "Aaaaagh!!!" I muffled a scream startled at the rattler I had almost stepped on. I froze. Nothing stirred, I heard no slithering or rattling, no excruciating pain. I needed to move or I would pass out. In slow motion and during what seemed to be hours, I flashed the beam of light where I remembered seeing the snake. He was still there, he hadn't moved. I stayed where I was trying to slow my breathing down so as not to frighten him. Mom wasn't going to have to kill me, I was already dead. I moved the flashlight down again, he hadn't moved. I peered at him, not moving a muscle. He was old, and where his eyes should have been there were gaping holes. His skin was shriveled around his coiled up skeleton. I exhaled realizing I had been holding my breath. The snake was dead.

I moved then, moved and grabbed hold of the railing track to scramble back out of the snake pit. I stretched my legs and pulled myself up, canteen slapping at my hip, flashlight tight in my clenched fist.

Wait 'til I tell Mom how I saw a dried up rattler in an abandoned mine she would, she would never know. I could not tell her because I would never be let out of her sight again.

I sat down on a big rock, breathing hard from my hasty climb, took a swig of the lukewarm canteen water and thought about the snake: scary, creepy, dried old beef jerky snake. It had died and been preserved by the heat, the dryness and the dust, even his rattle had stayed put. No one had been in that mine for years. So it **was** my mine and it needed a name. I named it, **Andy's Rattle Snake Mine.**

CHAPTER 4

I looked up at the sky, the sun had moved and I knew that if I wanted to be home before dark, I had better get going towards the Butte Mine. Mom had said we would have chicken fried steak and biscuits. I had about three hours before I needed to be headed back to the store.

I faced the direction of Red Mountain, it was no longer visible, but the bang, clank, bang clank was clear. Following the sound, I started walking.

I heard the noise of metal on metal before I saw the wooden sign *"Butte Mine"*. The clanking of the mining cart as it made its slow journey out of the gaping hole in the ground was audible even over the rhythmic banging. I could hear voices, deep, male mumblings that seemed to vibrate and echo out of the ground.

"Hey!" I called out as I approached the three men at work.

"Kid, whatcha doin here? Ain't no place here fer you."

His face was smudged with dirt and sweat had stained his worn t-shirt both under the arms and the big belly that bulged and hung over his faded jeans. He wasn't angry just irritated, like my Mom gets when I don't do my homework.

"Uh, I just walked here from Randsburg. Mr. Baker told me about the mine and I thought, well, I thought maybe I could learn how to find gold." I said confidently.

"Oh you did didya?" a tall, skinny, red haired man dressed in similar clothes to the big guy answered.

"Wadya think Joe, do we let kiddo stay?'

"My name's Andy, not kiddo," I said boldly.

"Feisty little kiddo you are too." said Red smiling, his teeth yellowed and stained with cigarette tar.

"What do you say, Jake? Does kiddo Andy stay or turn around and go home?"

Jake, muscles brown and glistening as he heaved a pick ax and shattered a large piece of quartz rock into smaller pieces, looked me over briefly and smiled.

"Where ya from Andy?" Jake asked.

"The Navy Base at China Lake," I answered proudly.

"Ridgecrest huh? Watcha doin' in Randsburg?"

"My Mom runs a knick knack shop."

Jake had turned back to his rock breaking. Joe was wheeling the barrow back towards the mine. Red winked and picked up the mortar and pestle at his feet, pulled up a wooden, three legged stool, sat down heavily and began crushing a piece of quartz. I watched quietly, no one had told me to go away. No one had asked me to stay either so I figured, if I were quiet, they wouldn't notice I was still there and I could learn how to find gold.

The two-stamp mill of John Quinn and George Pridham located two blocks from the center of town crushing 10 tons of quartz a day stopped its "bang, clank".

I looked down at Randsburg, saw some old charred buildings and remembered that Mom had told me about the two fires that had taken out the town, both in 1898. They had used dynamite to put out

the fires and that a small boy had been in one of the houses when it was about to be blown up. Quick action saved the boy. One other time, a hardware store full of merchandise, dishes and pans, was dynamited and the explosion caused a shower of plates, pots, pans and washtubs to rain down on that part of the town.

"That would have been something to see from up here! Look out below, you're about to get hit in the head with a washbasin!" I was thinking to myself and started laughing. The three miners looked up.

"C'mere boy, let me show ya sumpin." Red said, yellowed teeth showing as he spoke.
"See how I'ma grinding up this quartz?" I nodded.

"Now watch." He took a flat, metal, gold pan, shaped like a frying pan without a handle. He poured the dust into it. Next, he dipped the gold pan into the large wash pan filled with water. Slowly he poured the water into the gold pan. When the pan was full he carefully swirled the milky liquid allowing the contents to slosh over the edge back into the wash pan between his feet.

Once again he filled the gold pan with water, swirling carefully, in a clockwise direction, allowing the water to carry away the dissolved powder. He did this over and over until the pan held only clear water. He swirled the water and it circled the pan like liquid swirling down a partially clogged drain. Round and round the water went until the pan was almost empty and there at the bottom, glistening and bright were particles of gold dust.

"This here is gold, right out of this rock!"

My eyes grew large, gold, right there in front of my eyes had magically appeared out of the white, ground up quartz! He took a vial of glass and carefully tapped the gold specks into it. The vial was almost full!

"Wow! I wish I could learn to do that!" I blurted out.

"Ya do, do ya? Mmmm. Come back tomorrow and maybe we'll make a miner outta ya!" He laughed, pulled out of his sock a small cork stopper, inserted it in the vial and put it carefully into the right, deep pocket of his faded, dust encrusted, jeans.

"Thanks mister!" I said enthusiastically.

"The name's Red, Andy kiddo, that's Jake and that's Joe. It's getting late so come back tomorrow, early, ya hear? Sunrise."

"Yes, sir mister Red. Bye Jake, bye Joe."
I practically flew down the mountain, dodging rusted equipment, stumbling briefly on sliding rocks and found my way back to Randsburg and home.

CHAPTER 5

I had eaten my Mom's delicious chicken fried steak and biscuits quickly between my retelling of the afternoon. She smiled, pushing the strands of her brown hair away from her face. She still had most of it pulled back in a ponytail and she hadn't changed out of the pedal pusher shorts she'd worn on our trip here this morning. The morning seemed like days ago. My adventures with the tarantula and the rattlesnake were overshadowed by the gold and the miners.

My stomach gurgled as it worked on digesting the food I'd barely chewed; I turned from one position to another, wishing for sleep. I glanced at the clock, it was midnight and I was still awake. Soon it would be six and I could get up and get over to the Butte Mine.

I couldn't sleep. All I could think about was the gold at the bottom of Red's pan and how I was going to find my own gold and buy whatever I wanted. I stared at the ceiling watching the moonlight cast strange shadows as it found its way through my dusty windows. The evening was cool, cold almost, but it didn't matter, morning could not come soon enough.

CHAPTER 6

The sun was high in the sky by the time I woke up. It had been warming me as I lay passed out and exhausted on my bed. I was sweating from the heat and slow to move. The clock on the wall showed 9:45 am. Nine forty five! I was three hours late for my meeting with Red. I pulled on my jeans and a clean t-shirt, threw some water on my face and unruly hair, brushed most of my teeth and went in to the kitchen. Mom had left me a note.

> *"Andy, you looked so tired I let you sleep.*
> *Please hang clothes on the line outside, make*
> *yourself a sandwich, wait for Dr. Gordon for*
> *11:30 chess lesson."*

Awww! Now I was going to miss my chance to learn how to mine gold! I would go bright and early tomorrow. No wait, tomorrow was Sunday, the mine would be closed. Would Red teach me on Monday? Monday was two whole days away, how could I have not gotten up in time! I was so mad at myself! I pulled the clothes roughly out of the washer and threw them in a plastic laundry basket spilling the box of clothes pins all over the bottom. I took the wet clothes outside to the sagging clothes lines and hung them to dry, making sure I put two clothespins in each shirt and pair of jeans. I didn't want the wind to blow them off onto the dirt that constituted our back yard.

Back in the house I pulled out two pieces of Wonder Bread, a jar of Smucker's grape jelly from the fridge and a jar of peanut butter from the cabinet and put them on the green Formica table. I found a dirty knife in the sink, rinsed it off, dried it with a dish towel and made myself a PB and J. Jelly slid out of the bread in a big glob and I picked it up with two fingers and sucked it up. "Mmmm," my favorite sandwich was PB and J! I rinsed off my fingers and poured myself a generous glass of milk from the glass container on the top shelf of the fridge. I began feeling better, not so angry.

Dr. Gordon was my friend and had been teaching me things since I was little. He lived over in Johannesburg with his wife. Every Saturday, during the summer, he picked me up and taught me chess. Maybe he knew about gold mining. I glanced at the clock; it was already 11:30! The doorbell rang.

"Coming," I yelled out while quickly rinsing my dish with soap and water and puting it to dry. I took a sponge and ran it over the sticky stain on the table, threw it into the sink and ran for the door.

I opened the door. Dr. Gordon held a box full of violet bottles.

"Hello Andy, ready for some chess?"

"Sure," I replied, looking at the box, confused. "What are those empty bottles for?"

"Ah," he said as he walked in and put them on the kitchen table. "These are for your mother to sell."

"People buy old empty bottles?"

"These are special bottles, see the violet color?"

"Yeah," I said disinterestedly. "People pay money for old bottles?"

"Sure son, these bottles changed colors because manganese was used to make the glass this bottle was made from. People collect them; they even take old bottles and make bottle trees?"

"What's a bottle tree?"

"It's where bottles are put on sticks and exposed to the sun so that the manganese will change the color of the glass. They stopped putting manganese in glass in the 1930's, some of these bottles can be worth $100."

"A hundred dollars! For an old, ugly bottle? Where did you find them?"

"You can find them anywhere; people have been throwing out bottles for years. I found these near my house, I'm sure there are plenty of old bottles in the mine areas around here. You should keep your eyes open for them."

"I will, Mr. Gordon, thanks!"

We sat down to play a game of chess on an old board Dr. Gordon had brought and I told him all about the miners and the rattlesnake I had seen in the mine and about Red and Joe and Jake and the afternoon passed. I lost at chess but it was great to tell somebody about my adventures and know that he wouldn't get mad and he wouldn't tell Mom.

When Dr. Gordon left, I carried the bottles to Mom's shop and helped her put prices on them and set them up in a display. I looked at all the things she had painted. She had taught me to draw a little too and I liked it. When I grew up, I was going to study art.

The shop wasn't too busy and Mom gave me some money for a Nehi and a Moon Pie and I went to the

General Store. The sun was starting to work its way behind the mines and I could see the crest of Red Mountain blazing its brick red color. The wooden doors slammed behind me as I entered the shop.

"Well lookee here, its Andy kiddo. We missed you today son? Did you get confused and think it was Sunday?" Red asked as he chewed on a piece of licorice, his smile usually yellow now a black and yellow blur.

"I'm sorry Mister Red, sir, I'm really sorry. Can I come on Monday?"

"You still interested? Sure son, come on down whenever you can. We'll show you how to get some of this." He shook his vial of gold; it glistened in the last rays of light coming through the window. I watched as Mr. Beck poured the flecks of gold onto the scale, weighed it and counted out the money. Red folded the bills in half carefully and stuffed them deep into the front pocket of his dirt covered jeans.

I paid for my Moon Pie and drink and bit into the chocolate covered treat full of sticky marshmallow. Mmmm. The Nehi tickled my nose and the sticky treat stuck to my fingers and face. It had been a good day and Monday, I was going to find me some gold. I ran back to Mom's shop as she was locking up and together we walked down the dusty street towards our home. Mom was humming, her hair was loose, brown and shinny. I was almost as tall as she was.

"Pretty soon you'll be taller than I am," she said as if she'd read my mind.

"How tall will I be? As tall as Dad was?"

"Almost, as tall as your Dad, he was 6'4" and you'll be as handsome too," she said putting an arm around me and then quickly pulling back. "William Andrew Cherry, you are sticky and gooey! Go up and take a shower, brush your teeth and get to bed."

"Yes Ma'am," I said obediently, I was going to be early and getting out the door before the roosters crowed. Tomorrow was my lucky day, I felt it.

CHAPTER 7

My alarm rang at 5 am and I jumped out of bed, pulled on my jeans, an old t-shirt and a sweater to ward off the morning chill. It was cold in the kitchen and I poured myself a bowl of Corn Flakes, adding sugar and milk. I finished quickly, rinsed the bowl and spoon in the cold tap water and pulled on my Keds. After grabbing, an apple, my flashlight and canteen, I turned off the kitchen light and left quietly through the kitchen door.

It was dark and the wind ripped cold air through my sweater. I shivered and started to run to keep warm. I ran past the church, the school, up the hill, my flashlight bobbing wildly creating eerie shadows as it bounced off old abandoned machinery and dilapidated shacks. I could see the silhouette of the Butte Mine on the hill; it stood like a silent giant, dark and scary. I stopped to catch my breath, everything was too quiet. All I could hear was my breathing. Was that my breathing? I was frozen with fear, standing in the dark, on a hill alone. Finally, a light peeked through the mountains. It spread slowly, lighting the sky with ribbons of pink and yellow. The sun was rising. My breathing started to normalize and the "bang clank, bang, clank," started for the day. I could see the mine back lit by the sun. I started up the steep hill towards it.

I heard them before I saw them, their laughter and grumbling echoing through the mine and filtering down to me. Breathless, I climbed, taking long strides, approaching as quickly as my legs would allow.

"Morning Mister Red, Mister Jo, Mister Jake. I made it!" I said triumphantly panting and gasping for breath.

"Yer sure did kiddo, umm Andy."

"Git yerself some coffee."

"Uh, no thanks, I'm good."

Red laughed. He laughed so long he started coughing, he coughed and coughed and then he spit. His breath smelled of cigarettes.

"Okay boy, c'mer, I'm gonna give you a piece of quartz, you're gonna pound it in this mortar and pestle and then I'll show you again what to do. By then the sun will be full up and you'll be able to see if the rock had a gold vein."

The air was still chilly, my socks were thin, my toes freezing, I wiggled them in my Keds shoes as I sat down on a rock. With enthusiasm I picked up the quartz and hit it with the pestle, it shattered and I put a small piece in the mortar. I ground and ground it as I had remembered Red had done. It took me an hour to pulverize the quartz I had been given. Red came over occasionally to see how I was doing. I ground that pound of quartz until my hands hurt from holding the pestle. My arms felt like jelly from the constant force I had to apply. Sweat dripped from my forehead into my eyes and the salt and dirt stung. I got up when it was all a fine powder and put it in the gold pan. I put the gold pan in the larger water pan and swished.

"Whoa kiddo, you're going to lose the gold that way!" Red said warningly. He sauntered over and squatting beside me showed me how to get the water swirling and the white substance working its way out of the pan. I tried again, failing miserably at first and then finally getting the hang of it. As the cloudy liquid became clearer and heavy sediment settled at the bottom of the pan I felt my heart pounding in my chest. I saw something glimmer in the sunlight and I gave the pan a big swirl and swooshed it all into the big pan at my feet. My gold pan was now empty! In my haste I had dumped what little gold flecks I had gotten out of the quartz, into the big tub. Powdery quartz settled on top of it. The gold was gone.

"Noooo! Agh!" I yelled in despair. It was noon and I had nothing to show for my five hours of work. "I can't do this! It's dumb! A waste of time!"

"Calm down kiddo, if it were easy everybody would be doing it. That's why these machines were invented so that more quartz can be processed from the mine. You come back tomorrow and try again. Go home buddy, go play or read something or go eat. Forget about the gold, it ain't a life fer ya." I heard Jake's voice as if from a faraway place. I was in a disappointed daze. I got up slowly, licked my dry lips, wiped my eyes and nose on my sleeve and left without saying good-bye.

I went straight home, took a hot shower, ate a tuna sandwich Mom had made for me and left in the fridge with a note and went to see the comic book I couldn't buy.

The General Store was empty. Mr. Baker was asleep on the stool with his glasses perched on his nose and the newspaper in his hands. I walked back towards the magazine stand, picked the *Superman* comic up and turned it over, reading the back. Superman's Kryptonian name was Kal-El, his father's name was Jor-El, his cousin, Super girl, was Kara Zor-El. Andy-el. Sounded good. Mr. Baker stirred. I put the comic book back. I would start pounding quartz again tomorrow.

I went to the mine every day from dawn until dusk. I pounded quartz, coughed up dust, dirtied my clothes and finally was able to fill the vial with a tiny bit of gold. I was so happy. I had worked harder than I had ever worked.

"Good work, Andy kiddo, you have at least $20 worth of gold." Red said.

"Really? Are you sure?" I responded disbelievingly.

"Well, I'm not an expert and you know I don't have a scale but, well, go down and have Mr. Baker tell you." Red replied.

That afternoon, one week after I had started going to the mine, I ran to the General Store. The screen doors made a loud bang behind me. I strode over to the **Superman** comic book, picked it up and grabbed the Nehi from the refrigerator. I picked up and unwrapped a Moon Pie stuffing half of it into my mouth before I made it to the register.

"Andy! So you have some money today!" Mr. Baker said looking a little worried.

"Better. I have something to pay for all of this." I pulled out my small vial and placed it on the counter.

"Lookee here," Mr. Baker held the vial up and eyed the gold. "You got just enough for your comic, that half eaten Moon Pie and an extra Moon Pie," the store owner said handing me a second

Moon Pie. He put his hand in his pocket, his fingers searched inside and he took out a handful of coins. With his other hand he plucked out two quarters and a nickel, looked at them and then opened the cash register and dropped them in their respective places. He put my gold vial in his pocket.

"Thank you son. Have a nice evening and enjoy your comic book."

The gooey Moon Pie stuck to the roof of my mouth. I guess Red was wrong, I hadn't found a lot of gold. Had I?

Randsburg, CA February 2010

54

Soda fountain in General Store, Randsburg.

What's left of the Butte Mine

Violet, glass bottle made with manganese

Large quartz boulders in Randsburg, CA

Quartz pieces with veins of gold

ABOUT THE AUTHOR

Georgette Baker was born on the island of Aruba raised in Venezuela and lived in Ecuador and Greece. She speaks five languages and is the author of the bilingual children's travel/animal books, "We're Off..." She is the producer of the bilingual children's music series *Cantemos*. Georgette currently resides in Southern California and gives presentations in schools and libraries. This is her first chapter book for children.

http://www.cantemosco.com